Praise for The Social Justice

"SJWs are vital to the movement. Wl... SJWs will start smashing storefronts, seeing 'microaggressions' everywhere, demanding college dormitories change their names to create a 'safe space,' or some other idea that annoys everybody. Get *The Social Justice Warrior Handbook* and be happy every day!"
— Ann Coulter, Twelve-Time *New York Times* Bestselling Author

"As a former Army Special Forces and combat guy, I can tell you there is no greater cause than the fight for your right to be comfortable at all times. Lisa De Pasquale gives SJWs the respect they deserve."
— Terry Schappert, Canine Parent

"*The Social Justice Warrior Handbook* is an invaluable tool for the modern LGBTQIA activist desperate to fight the oppression of pronouns and gender specific bathrooms all while ignoring the barbaric treatment of LGBT people in the Islamic world!"
— Chris R. Barron, Gay Activist

"Thanks to decades of less than diverse content from Marvel and DC Comics there are dozens of beloved characters to culturally re-appropriate and gender flip. *The Social Justice Warrior Handbook* is Virtue Signaling made easy."
— Brett R. Smith, Comic Book Artist and *New York Times* Bestselling Author, co-author of *Thump*

"When it comes to political advice, you should only listen to Hollywood actors like me, but if I'm unavailable, this book will do."
— Nick Searcy, Peabody Award-winning International Film and Television Star

"I used my white male privilege to be quoted in this book."
— Andrew Schulz, Comedian

THE
SOCIAL JUSTICE
WARRIOR
HANDBOOK

A Practical Survival Guide for
Snowflakes, Millennials, and Generation Z

Lisa De Pasquale

A POST HILL PRESS BOOK
ISBN: 978-1-68261-479-2
ISBN (eBook): 978-1-68261-480-8

The Social Justice Warrior Handbook:
A Practical Survival Guide for Snowflakes, Millennials, and
Generation Z
© 2017 by Lisa De Pasquale
All Rights Reserved

Cover Design by Tricia Principe, triciaprincipedesign.com

Post Hill Press
New York • Nashville
posthillpress.com

Published in the United States of America

JUL 2 0 2019

ACKNOWLEDGMENTS

I'll always cherish the time I spent traveling to college campuses across the country and being among the Social Justice Warriors, snowflakes, and millennials because Floyd Resnick was usually with me. *The Social Justice Warrior Handbook* is dedicated to him because I think it would have made him laugh and boy, do I miss his laugh.

I am very grateful to those who endorsed this book: Chris Barron, Ann Coulter, Terry Schappert, Andrew Schulz, Nick Searcy, and Brett Smith.

Thank you to those who have encouraged me or inspired me through their works while writing this book: Scott Adams, Mike Baker, Nick Gillespie, Greg Gutfeld, Christie Herrera, Thaddeus McCotter, Gavin McInnes, Scott Mitchell, Mike Rowe, Ben Shapiro, and Kat Timpf.

Sincere thanks to Post Hill Press for the freedom to write a fun, political book. Extra-special thanks to Ivan for his wonderful illustrations.

Finally, I am thankful to God for giving me the opportunity to write this book and meet all the amazing people who helped along the way.

"Within every joke is a tiny revolution."
–George Orwell

TABLE OF CONTENTS

SECTION 1

Becoming a

Social Justice Warrior

YOUR SJW IDENTITY

We live in a complex, problematic world. Every day we see people driving their cars, going to their jobs, spending time with their friends and families. They are oblivious to how they contribute to the problems in America.

Enter the Social Justice Warrior.

For too many years the word "warrior" has been co-opted by militaristic cultures. The term "warrior" has been used to describe people—usually cisgender men—who adhered to a severe code of conduct and trained for a period of time to develop skills using weapons and fighting. This narrow definition of "warrior" no longer fits with modern society. By purchasing this book, you've taken the first step in training to be a Social Justice Warrior. This book will unlock the secrets to building your skills in identifying social injustice and surviving in a world that doesn't care about your feelings—but should. The power to change your school, your neighborhood, your workplace, your country, and *the world* is at your fingertips.

[Author's Note: By using the word "fingertips" I don't wish to communicate an ableist viewpoint that one must have fingers to be a warrior.]

Being a Social Justice Warrior has many rewards. You get to educate people on how they can be better human beings. It takes a special, unique person to be a Social Justice Warrior. Before endeavoring on this journey to become an expert in social justice, you must first figure out what kind of warrior you are. Many of these overlap, so be sure to claim superiority using the label that signals your virtue the most. Most importantly, don't force an identity on yourself. Journal your feelings, experiment, then decide which identity feels the most natural to you that day. Your Social Justice Warrior identity is completely fluid.

Feminist

Are you uncomfortable when men view you as a sex object?

Are you offended when men don't find you sexually attractive because of your hair, lack of femininity, odor, clothing, or demeanor?

Do you assert your independence by demanding the government pay for your life choices?

Does a stranger suggesting you smile send you into a fit of rage? Don't just act—ovary-act.

Unlike our grandmothers, mothers, and professors, being a feminist doesn't mean burning your bra. It means demanding that everyone look at you *in* your bra. Being a feminist activist is the most freeing thing you can do because *you* make the rules and *you* are now the majority. Studies show that more American women receive college degrees than men, so you already have a built-in community that's eager to capitulate to your demands.

There is no such thing as a stereotypical feminist. This is because women across the country are oppressed in new and unique ways despite social norms that have virtually eliminated sex discrimination.

Declaring that you're a feminist is the most important aspect of the movement. Here are some items every feminist needs to help ignite the fight for social justice:

- "We Should All Be Feminists" t-shirt, $710, available at Dior Boutiques and online

- If Dior's inspiring shirt is not in your budget, there are many others available with irreverent, inspiring sayings like:
  - "Nasty Gal"
  - "A Woman's Place is in the House and the Senate"
  - "Love Trumps Hate"
  - "Fuck Ann Coulter"
  - "No Uterus, No Opinion"
  - "Pro-Feminist Is Not Anti-Men"
- Books written by relatable and diverse role models like Lena Dunham, Chelsea Clinton, Amy Schumer, Elizabeth Warren, Tina Fey, Chelsea Handler, and Samantha Bee
- If you choose to wear make-up, look for brands that use empowering messages like "Slay, bitch!" and "Be your own kind of beautiful."

Being a modern feminist is about defying the negative stereotypes the hetero-patriarchy has imposed on us. Popular vlogger and feminist ally Miles McInnes has been supportive of taking back words like "bitch." During the 2016 presidential election, Miles pointed out that Hillary Clinton was a "bad ass bitch." He said, "What did she do with Benghazi? They said 'Hey we need help over here.' She said, 'Screw you.' She was a total bitch about it. Then, when a bunch of people died, she said, 'What difference does it make?' What a super cool bitch."

Since Miles McInnes is an ally and very effective advocate for the Social Justice Warrior movement, it's ok for him to use our word. However, anyone who wore a "Trump That Bitch" t-shirt during the campaign is basically guilty of a hate crime.

[Author's Note: I should point out that Miles McInnes is the brother of Gavin McInnes, a so-called "libertarian family man." Gavin is *not* a friend to feminists.]

Workplace Warrior

If you have a career and regular paycheck, you may think that you can't be a Social Justice Warrior. Wrong! Too often people think that because they work in a traditional office they aren't able to contribute to the movement. In fact, the workplace is ripe for reform because it brings together people from outside your comfort zone who may not be aware of how their seemingly innocuous behavior is actually trampling on other people's rights.

As a Workplace Warrior, you can educate your coworkers on how words like "postman" and "chairman" set women's rights back fifty years, or why "Taco Tuesday" is insulting to the one person in your office who looks like zie (A.B.G.N.—Always Be Gender Neutral) might be Hispanic.

Your coworkers will be grateful for the learning opportunities you present to them.

As a Workplace Warrior, you can also affect your coworkers and change the office culture in subtle ways:

- Rather than approach a coworker who posted a photo on social media showing Trump at a local event, speak to your Human Resources representative privately about how this fosters a hostile work environment for those who didn't vote for Trump.
- Bring a batch of raw, non-GMO, gluten free, vegan protein bites to the next staff meeting (See SJWHandbook.com for the recipe).
- Show your political personality with a BPA-free water bottle printed with the saying "Republican Tears."
- Ride your bike to work and make sure your bike helmet is visible on your desk while you talk about your low carbon footprint.
- Suggest the office thermostat is set at seventy-eight degrees during the summer to lower your corporate carbon footprint.
- On casual Friday, pair a nice blazer with a "Democrats give a sh*t about people" t-shirt, available from the Democratic National Committee.

Social Media Warrior

The Social Justice Warrior movement's forerunners (this is the proper gender-neutral term) did not have the incredible opportunities we now have through social media. As a Social Media Warrior you have direct access to the media and politicians. Better still, you can take the racists, misogynists, homophobes, and bigots to task in real time. Just imagine the looks on their faces when you retweet an offensive tweet and add the comment, "Delete your account." BOOM!

One benefit of being a Social Media Warrior is that you can represent hordes of other people who don't have the courage or privilege to engage with top-selling brands about their every marketing decision. Have you ever seen a married couple in a commercial and the husband didn't appear to be a bumbling fool giving in to his wife? It's the perfect opportunity to tweet to the company and ask why the company doesn't feature a trans, gay, or interracial couple instead. There are also endless opportunities to hound brands that advertise on sites that are offensive to you.

On January 7, 2017, the *New York Times* published an article titled, "How to Destroy the Business Model of Breitbart and Fake News." Then on March 26, 2017, they published an article titled "Brands Try to Blacklist Breitbart, But Ads Slip Through Anyway." It was a reminder that we must always be vigilant. It's also important to note that the number of social media followers you have isn't an indication of whether your concerns are valid. In the *New York Times* March article, they highlighted the complaints of a Social Media Warrior who had only twenty-five followers. As a result, multimillion dollar brands reflexively pulled their ads from a high-traffic website.

Professional Protestor

In the 1960s people met at community centers and churches to plan protests. They often traveled in buses to other locations to demonstrate against segregation and other important civil rights issues. Like Social Media Warriors, today's Professional Protestors are able to organize and demonstrate because of the internet. As a Professional Protestor, you can travel across the country, receive compensation, and you don't even have to make your own signs because they're usually printed and provided by the protest sponsor. Shirts, too!

Craigslist is a great resource for finding opportunities to hone your skills as a Social Justice Warrior. For example, there was a Craigslist post from a progressive organization called Grassroots Campaigns looking for "face-to-face outreach" that pays "$7,040–$9,600 for the summer" to help "fight for comprehensive reproduction education" in schools. Don't worry; just because the organization is headquartered in Washington, D.C., doesn't mean opportunities aren't available in a city near you (or a city you want to travel to during the summer). Just on this one issue, they are seeking field operatives (a better way to say "protestor" on your resume) in Amherst, MA; Boston MA; New York, NY; Philadelphia, PA; Raleigh-Durham, NC; Charlotte, NC; Chicago, IL; Kansas City, MO, New Orleans, LA; Austin, TX; Boulder, CO; Denver, CO; Seattle, WA; Berkeley, CA; Los Angeles, CA; Sacramento, CA; and San Diego, CA.

If you think that not having children in the public school system matters, don't worry. One advantage of the Social Justice Warrior movement is that we are called to speak out on a multitude of issues even if they don't affect us directly.

Entertainer

Many Social Justice Warrior categories overlap, and that's certainly the case with being an Entertainer. However, Entertainers are among the most useful warriors because they have bigger platforms to bring awareness and change, while also appealing to a younger demographic.

For older Entertainers, dipping a toe in the waters of social justice will help you gain media attention. It's especially helpful for older actresses who want media exposure from hipper sites like *Refinery29* and *Teen Vogue*. For younger entertainers, particularly young actresses who want to make the jump from coming-of-age-lose-your-virginity-before-the-school-year-ends movies to serious roles that include complicated lesbian relationships or rape scenes, any issue related to sex is an excellent place to begin. These might include:

- Reproductive rights
- Trans rights (or gay rights if you're from a Southern state because that's still edgy enough; ask your makeup or hair stylists for their thoughts so you're up to date on the latest terms)

- Your looks (if you're a classic beauty, demand interviewers ask you more than what you're wearing. If you're not conventionally attractive, demand interviewers ask you about challenging beauty standards.)

One of the most impactful and humble ways you can share your virtue is by posting a selfie while wearing a social justice message t-shirt. Go without professionally applied make-up and dozens of publications will call you #brave.

If you're an actor, perhaps one with a wild past, you can rehabilitate your image with female fans and Democratic politicians longing for relevance by speaking out on these issues:

- Climate change (a must if you're frequently seen on private jets)
- Equal pay for women costars
- Confederate flag (cross-promotion opportunities if you play a racist Southerner in a movie)
- Gay rights (if you've ever played a gay or questioning character, you'll automatically have authority on this issue)
- Increasing minimum wage (talk about those six months you were a waiter or worked construction before getting your big break)

If you don't want to commit to a specific issue, always remember that playing the downtrodden shows that you have a special connection to their struggles, perhaps more so because you can better appreciate the difference between their lives and the lives of privileged entertainers.

PRO TIP

*"This is one giant Live Action Role Play ...
You are safe."*

-Former Green Beret and Master Sergeant in the
U.S. Army Special Forces Terry Schappert

SECTION 2

Your Social Justice Warrior
Survival Guide

HOW TO CREATE YOUR SAFE SPACE

Now that you've accepted the responsibility of speaking for the defenseless and speaking out against the small-minded people who disagree with you, it's time to create a space that fosters your productivity and creativity. This doesn't have to be a private space. It could be your school, your workplace, a city street, the apartment you share, or even a restaurant you might pass.

Everyone's idea of a safe space is different. UC-Berkeley alum Greg Gutfeld said, "For those who flee to villas of victimhood never learn conflict resolution and will flunk in the real world. The real world is no safe space."

So, you must make it one.

An organization called Women Win created the definitive guide on creating emotional and physical safe spaces. They "gathered a diverse set of experts, coaches, programme directors and girls from around the world to share their knowledge about how to address gender-based violence through sport."

While their guide is intended for women, there are some good suggestions that Social Justice Warriors of any gender can implement in public and private spaces. From the Women Win's guide:

- "Ensure that girls have adequate protective gear for sports that require it." [Author's Note: This may include jockstraps.]
- "Establish the rules of the game girls are playing and enforce fair play."

- "Consider holding sessions in spaces that can be physically enclosed, to keep outsiders out and to help girls feel secure."
- "Allow girls to speak about sensitive topics in the language that is most comfortable. However, be aware that girls who do not speak the majority language may feel marginalized."
- "Provide private changing rooms. Although a permanent girls-only space is preferable, it is fine to use a space to change that is used by both men and women, as long as boys are prohibited from entering during the time girls are using it. In conservative cultures, it may be necessary to establish same-sex spaces and/or clothing accommodations to ensure girls are comfortable." [Author's Note: The terms "boy" and "girl" can be determined by the child at any time.]

These rules were written for children, but as adults we should also help create safe spaces for ourselves and for others. A safe space is one that doesn't question our views, values, or self-esteem. This is especially true on a college campus because it's a place where we should be free to explore ourselves. The Safe Space Network says, "A Safe Space is a place where anyone can relax and be able to fully express, without fear of being made to feel uncomfortable, unwelcome, or unsafe on account of biological sex, race/ethnicity, sexual orientation, gender identity or expression, cultural background, religious affiliation, age, or physical or mental ability."

To create a public safe space, be sure it is free from:

- People who have publicly or privately disagreed with that cool professor who sometimes has class outside
- White cisgender men who don't identify as feminists
- White cisgender women who don't identify as feminists
- People of color who aren't progressives

- Flyers or other propaganda advertising events or speeches associated with College Republicans or other right-wing groups
- Cultural appropriation; it's offensive to use another culture's tradition because you appreciate it or it's "trendy"

In addition to creating safe public spaces, you should also create a safe personal space in your residence. A residence can be a dorm, a loft apartment with exposed brick, the guest bedroom, or basement in your parents' house because it really should be separate from your bedroom, or even a room in a house or apartment you share with a partner.

Creating a safe space in your home is about comfort. One way to achieve it is to embrace the Danish tradition of *hygge* (pronounced *hoo-guh*). *The Oxford Dictionary* describes hygge as "a quality of coziness and comfortable conviviality that engenders a feeling of contentment or well-being." It is derived from a 16th century Norwegian term meaning "to comfort." *The New Yorker* describes hygge as "candles, nubby woolens, shearling slippers, woven textiles, pastries, blond wood, sheepskin rugs, lattes with milk-foam hearts, and a warm fireplace."

PRO TIP

"The ultimate safe space is a coffin."

-UC-Berkeley Alum Greg Gutfeld

HOW TO LIVE IN YOUR PARENTS' HOME WITH DIGNITY AND CONDESCENSION

The downside of being a Social Justice Warrior is that often the world doesn't value your efforts. Being a Social Justice Warrior might not be immediately lucrative, but it eventually will be, with tenure, speaking fees, and diversity administrator titles. It may be necessary for you to live with your parents until you find your niche in the Social Justice Warrior movement. It's also an opportunity to lecture an older generation on their privilege while living under their roof.

In 2017, the U.S. Census Bureau reported that one in three people between the ages of 18 and 34 are living with their parents rather than alone or with a spouse, partner, or roommate. That's the highest percentage in decades. Additionally, a survey by TD Ameritrade found that almost half of college graduates plan to move home after graduation in order to offset the cost of high student loan payments.

Living at home after college is the new normal, so there is no reason to be ashamed or apologize for it. In fact, your parents should be happy to have you home so you can educate them about social justice and low-key racism. Now that you're educated and cultured, perhaps more than they are, they should be open to your views.

Their Professions/Privilege

Since you operate on a higher level of social awareness and read news sources they don't, you can tell them the truth about the industry in which they work and how it is affecting the environment or those at a lower economic level.

Their Vehicles

When they periodically leave the house to go to work or, if retired, run errands and go to social events, let them know that the summer they paid for your trip abroad you found that Europeans are much more environmentally responsible than Americans. Everyone uses public transportation or a bicycle.

Their Food

Since your parents most likely do the bulk of the grocery shopping, don't miss an opportunity to stand in front of the pantry or refrigerator and offer advice on their food choices. (Go ahead and still eat their food. You don't want to be insulting.)

Fox News Channel

After a few days of living at home, you may notice that your parents often have Fox News on TV (bless their hearts for still having cable or satellite!). Your mom may try to diffuse the conversation by saying, "It's only on for background noise" or "I just like that Dana Perino and her dog, Jasper." Be sure to comment on the female hosts' clothing while dismissing anything they say. If a black, Hispanic, or gay conservative is on the screen, point out that they are a traitor to their people and the hard work Social Justice Warriors like you do every day. Also, call attention to the racist and sexist views of the white male hosts and guests.

Rent

At some point the topic of paying rent may come up, especially if you receive a regular paycheck. To avoid this expense, you should periodically remind your parents of your value around the house. Water plants when they're out of town. Help clear out their pantry and refrigerator of foods that don't fit your food philosophy. Fill their DVR with shows that will expand their cultural and political views, like *Real Time with Bill Maher*, *The Daily Show with Trevor Noah*, *Empire*, and *RuPaul's Drag Race*. Remind them of your student loan debt. Bring around friends who also live at home, but who are less successful.

HOW TO CREATE YOUR AUTHENTIC VINTAGE STYLE

An important aspect of communicating our ideas and message is through our personal styles and vibe. Social Justice Warrior style is about looking authentic and unique. There are many mass-market retailers that cater to our tastes. In fact, designers look to us for what's on-trend.

Here are some items you'll want to incorporate into your wardrobe:

Millennial Pink

This is not your mother's shade of pink. In fact, it's more like your grandmother's shade of pink. Millennial pink isn't pink "on steroids" (a phrase those marketing to GenXers used a lot). Millennial pink is pink on pot. It's mellow, dusty, faded, and co-opted as our own. Best of all, it's suitable for all sixty-three genders.

According to *Slate* magazine, "Millennial pink is the Elizabeth Warren of colors—no matter how tired we are of hearing about it, it persists."

Millennial pink is a streetwear staple. No Instagram filter required (well, maybe Mayfair or 1977). Marlien Rentmeester, founder of *Le Catch*, said, "We interpret our environment through the colors we wear. Pink is unapologetic, dramatic, and bold. We're taking it back and making it our own."

Laurie Pressman, vice president of the Pantone Color Institute said, "A color becomes popular because it's symbolic of the age we're living in. These are turbulent times. People are looking for calm." Carrying the torch for social justice can be stressful. Millennial pink is like a warm, cozy, gender-neutral baby blanket.

Band and Concert Tees

History began the day we were born. Unfortunately, that means a majority of the concerts we actually attended as teenagers were Britney Spears, NSYNC, Fallout Boy, and Taylor Swift. While it is possible to wear their shirts ironically, you'll be better off curating your look with older bands.

Acceptable Bands

- NWA, Ice-T, Wu Tang Clan, other classic rap artists
- Pink Floyd, Led Zeppelin, REM, Nirvana, other classic rock bands
- Blondie, Joan Jett, The Runaways, and other badass women
- Sex Pistols, The Ramones, The Clash, Misfits, Motörhead

Unacceptable Bands

- Country artists because they're usually associated with right-wingers (Please note that despite the Dixie Chicks speaking out against George W. Bush, the word "Dixie" is offensive)
- "Hair" bands because their misogynistic videos are degrading and problematic

- KISS because of misogynistic lyrics and Gene Simmons supported Donald Trump in the 2016 presidential election

You can buy t-shirts that are weathered, but for real authenticity you should do it yourself.

TOOLS YOU'LL NEED

- Scissors
- Bleach
- Sandpaper
- Tea bags

Using these tools you can customize your t-shirts. You can distress the images by gently rubbing sandpaper on them. You can mellow light colors by soaking them in warm water with teabags. This also works with books you want people to think you've had for a long time! You can lighten black t-shirts by soaking them in a solution of three parts water and one part bleach, then washing and drying them. You can create a casual, off-the-shoulder look by cutting a wider neckline. If you're a woman or a man without muscle definition, create a badass/I-don't-give-a-fuck look by cutting off the shirtsleeves. If you're a man with muscle definition, avoid this as it contributes to toxic masculinity.

Distressed Denim

Like t-shirts, there are plenty of options when it comes to distressed denim—persimmon-dyed, ripped, repaired-ripped, sandblasted, beet-dyed, bleached, destroyed, and shredded, among others. To preserve your distressed denim, don't wash them and ignore your coworkers, classmates, or roommates if they complain about the odor.

PRPS, a New York-based designer, offers a wide array of distressed denim for men and women, including overalls, jackets, tops, and bottoms. The pieces are ripped and some include synthetic mud and paint for a faux-authentic blue-collar look. Their most well known jeans is the Barracuda Straight Leg Jeans. Nordstrom's describes it this way, "Heavily distressed medium-blue denim jeans in a comfortable straight-leg fit embody rugged, Americana workwear that's seen some hard-working action with a crackled, caked-on muddy coating that shows you're not afraid to get down and dirty."

Whether canvassing a neighborhood on behalf of subsidies for solar power corporations or protesting against an Orthodox Jewish speaker like Ben Shapiro, distressed denim is a must-have for showing your concern for the oppressed.

The Barracuda Straight Leg Jeans retail at $425.

PRO TIP

"It is a fashion, a way of life. Inspired by the very homeless, the vagrants, the crack whores that make this wonderful city so unique."

–Fashion Designer Jacobim Mugatu

Accessories and Other Finishing Touches

Goodwill and other thrift stores are excellent resources to complete your look. Build a collection of worn-in work boots, scarves, canvas tote bags, and books. If you feel like a poser for buying second-hand clothes, feel free to embellish. No, not with rhinestones—with a story!

Maybe that flannel work shirt belonged to a farmer. It could have been your dead grandfather's for all you know. Giving a clothing item a backstory gives it authenticity.

Ethical Fashion

While not vintage, ethical fashion is an important part of a Social Justice Warrior's wardrobe. It is a term used for clothing that's vegan (no leather), made using fair trade policies, by workers receiving a living wage, and produced with sustainable materials, among other things. As a Social Justice Warrior, you are obligated to tell every single person when you are wearing an ethically produced item of clothing and educate them on why their clothing is worse than Hitler.

HOW TO PACK A SOCIAL JUSTICE WARRIOR GO-BAG

After the election of Donald Trump (#NotMyPresident) in 2016 there is a real possibility that there will be a need to survive on our own because basic social and survival needs will be cut off, especially for the Social Justice Warriors who have spoken truth to power on Twitter, Facebook, college campuses, all forms of media, and at Hollywood awards shows.

PRO TIP

"A Bug-Out-Bag is sometimes referred to as a B-O-B. But, it really depends on how your bag self-identifies. I think burdening your kit with a gender specific name might create more baggage than the typical SJW is willing to carry."

```
-Former CIA Covert Operations Officer
           Mike Baker
```

A go-bag or bug-out-bag is filled with necessities that will help you survive when evacuating from an environmental disaster (likely caused by climate change), martial law ordered by a Republican administration, or an event like Coachella or FyreFest. There has been a lot of chatter on social media about the need for a go-bag or bug-out bag. Here are some quotes from real people on Twitter (not using their Twitter handle so they won't be targeted by right-wingers):

"My 9 y/o sister made a bug out bag bec she's afraid that we're all going to die now that Trump is president"

"Preparing for President Trump: turning every pocket I own into a Go-bag"

"Tomorrow we'll be making a Bug Out Bag in Trump's America."

"I know I am prepping my bug out bag. #TRUMP"

"I have a Trump go-bag ready."

"I've officially turned into a 'prepper'. Been working on my bug-out-bag, reading Army manual, and everything. Thanks Trump!"

"my mom and i already have our trexit* strategy in place, and i will have a go-bag at the door for nov 9th

(* = trump wins, i exit)"

"Better make sure you have your supply's and bug out bag ready. #Trump the new #y2k. #y2k17"

"50 Items You Forgot To Put In Your Bug Out Bag snip. ly/3gzc6 #trump #orlando #genocide"

"As if trump is president. I'm prepping a bug out bag because the world will go to shit tbh"

"If the election goes to Trump today I'm making myself a bug out bag and becoming a survivalist"

There are several pre-packed go-bags available, but those aren't ideal for Social Justice Warriors. A go-bag is not just the opportunity to share your identity, but to also share your knowledge on social justice and ethical survival to the captive audience around you.

PRO TIP

"Your go-bag doesn't want to become a go-rucksack because it's huge and unwieldy. You're going to stop carrying it around because it's just a pain in the butt. You want to really condense this down to the essential things you could use."

–Former Green Beret and Master Sergeant in the U.S. Army Special Forces Terry Schappert

Go-Bag Essentials

WATER

- Use a container made from BPA-free, recyclable materials
- Survival situations can be stressful, so as a treat also consider packing sparkling water such as LaCroix, Whole Foods

Italian Sparkling Water, Hal's New York Seltzer Water, or Perrier
- Survival experts may tell you to keep a couple iodine tabs to purify water from unknown sources, but I'm skeptical of adding chemicals to water

FOOD

- You want to carry light items that aren't filled with toxins
- Jerky comes in many forms, including free-range meat products, seitan, and tofu
- Non-GMO snacks such as fruit leathers and energy bars
- Greenpeace gives many of the most popular brands of tuna a low grade for ethics and sustainability, so be sure to check out their recommendations before packing your food rations
- A couple bottles of liquor or organic Moscato

COMMUNICATIONS

- Smartphone with charger and durable case
- Extra battery packs for smartphone
- Ear buds/headphones
- Kickstand to watch movies
- Pen and paper (*trés* retro!)

MEDICINES/FIRST AID

- Pain relievers
- Vitamins (there are many vegan gummy vitamins available)
- Any prescriptions, hormones, or THC-laced edibles for anxiety that you take on a regular basis
- A basic first aid kit that includes sterilized bandages, Plan B One-Step®, antibiotic ointment, tweezers, and hand sanitizer

PRO TIP

"Most folks will advise you to have food/water/ emergency material to get you through a 72-hour period. My advice is... think bigger. Think about how much weed and matcha tea you go through at your typical music festival, or multi-day drum circle, and then multiply by three or four times. We are talking about supplies to get you through a major crisis. And don't forget a spare hacky sack."

−Former CIA Covert Operations Officer
Mike Baker

Miscellaneous Items

- Vaporizer and accessories (try some fun e-liquids such as Unicorn Milk, Essence of Che, Zombie Blood, Goblin Goo, Cuban Cigar, and Hillary's Hot Sauce)
- Lighter (in case you need to light up a storefront or police car)
- A book to help keep your spirits up
- Extra socks, which can also pull double-duty as mittens
- Safety scissors or spork (a knife is too aggressive in an already stressful situation)
- Multitool with a wine bottle opener
- *The Social Justice Warrior Handbook*, of course

Items to Avoid

- Compass, GPS, flashlight, family photos, maps, camera (all of these items are already on your phone and will just add unnecessary bulk to your go-bag)
- MREs (people might think you're part of the military industrial complex)
- Birth control and condoms, as the government should provide these for free

WHAT TO DO WHEN SOMEONE ASSUMES YOUR GENDER

Gender and sexual identity is a personal matter and no longer a construct of outdated social norms. As a Social Justice Warrior, it's your duty to educate people by immediately making them aware of your gender preferences. This author believes in practicing what she preaches given her cis privilege. I am a cisgender, heterosexual woman who is attracted to cisgender men in their late 40s and early 50s who display toxic masculinity. In interviews about this and my other writings, you may refer to me by using my personal pronouns of "her" and "she."

In early 2014, Social Justice Warriors were successful in getting Facebook to list fifty-eight gender options. Thankfully, Facebook's diversity team has now made gender unlimited. From Facebook Diversity:

Last year we were proud to add a custom gender option to help people better express their identities on Facebook. We collaborated with our Network of Support, a group of leading LGBT advocacy organizations, to offer an extensive list of gender identities that many people use to describe themselves. After a year of offering this feature, we have expanded it to include a free-form field.

Now, if you do not identify with the pre-populated list of gender identities, you are able to add your own. As before, you can add up to ten gender terms and also have the ability to control the audience with whom you would like to share your custom gender. We recognize that some people face challenges sharing their true gender identity with others, and this setting gives people the ability to express themselves in an authentic way.

The expanded custom gender option is available to everyone who uses Facebook in US English.

Clearly, there is still work to be done on behalf of those who don't use Facebook in US English. Still, you'll find that the real world is not as gender-inclusive as Facebook and every day there will be assumptions about your gender. According to the website *Everyday Feminism*, assuming another person's gender is "rude, and can cause a lot of harm. If you assume, you're saying that you think you know someone else better than they know themselves."

Here are some sample scripts to help you deal with everyday situations. Remember that as a Social Justice Warrior you operate on a much higher plane of awareness, so you should still be polite to the offender.

At a Restaurant

Server: Hello ladies, are you ready to order?

You: Actually, we don't use gender-specific words like "ladies."

Server: Um, okay.

You: Please use gender-neutral words such as "they" and "their."

Server: Are they ready to order?

You: Is your triple-decker burger grass-fed, organic, and locally raised?

First Day of School

Teacher: Has anyone seen Julie? Her desk is empty.

You: We haven't met Julie yet, so we don't know her personal pronoun.

Teacher: The name I have is Julie, so...

You: You use the proper gender-neutral zie/zim/zir until zie arrives so as not to offend other classmates or zir during zir absence.

Planning a Coworker's Fetus Shower

Coworker: She said she's having a boy, so I thought we could decorate the conference room with blue balloons.

You: We actually don't know the fetus's gender identity, so we should use a color that doesn't follow traditional gender roles.

Coworker: What color should we use?

You: Oatmeal.

CHOOSING YOUR FOOD PHILOSOPHY

Your food philosophy is almost as important as your Social Justice Warrior identity. Food brings people together in a non-aggressive setting. It's a good way to introduce principles of social justice while friends and family just want to enjoy their meals.

The first rule of any food philosophy is that you must always talk about your food philosophy. You might think that going vegan is the best option, but that's not necessarily true. Your food philosophy helps nurture your identity. It's a conversation starter and one that should counter the dominant culture in your city or group of friends. You know about raw, vegan, vegetarian, pescatarian, farm-to-table, and other trendy food philosophies. Here are some others to explore.

Nose to Tail

If you live in California or other progressive location, consider a food philosophy that incorporates locally raised, organically fed, noncommodity animals. Embrace the offal! Offal are the organs and entrails of animals. You may receive some judgment from friends on the vegetarian spectrum, but remind them that using and respecting the entire animal is part of the Native American tradition, as well as a necessity in other cultures. For example, many Native Americans boiled the full stomachs of buffalo for a tasty grass stew. In modern society, this might include foie gras or pâté prepared by a chef with a tattoo of a butchered pig diagram. If you are a committed vegetarian or vegan, you can instead describe your food philosophy as "root to leaf."

Political Fasting

Political Fasting is a great way to bring attention to social injustice. In April 2017, Yale University graduate teachers held a symbolic fast in support of unionization. Some only ate when hungry. Others took turns fasting. Others fasted until they were "medically unable" to continue.

Detoxing

Detoxing is a great way to rid your body of toxins and show your friends and family that you can afford expensive shakes, juices, and supplements. *Goop*, founded by Gwyneth Paltrow, recommends Dr. Junger's 21-Day Clean Plan. The Plan includes a 21-day supply of supplements, shake mixes, and probiotics for $475. Recipes for your one "clean" meal per day (lunch) are included, but the food is not. By no means should you avoid social gatherings during your detox. Going to restaurants, bars, and dinner parties during a detox is the perfect opportunity to tell people about this expensive inconvenience you've brought on yourself, and to describe in detail the benefits of regular colonics.

PRO TIP

"Grumbleflaunting: When you invent some silly nit to pick in order to broadcast that you have access to elite goods like First Class."

-Blogger Ace of Spades

Nostalgic Eating

The stress of being a Social Justice Warrior in today's problematic world can be overwhelming. You can find comfort in nostalgic foods from the past. If you're still living at home, ask your mom or dad to leave dishes you enjoyed as a child so you can reheat at your convenience. (For the recipe for my mom's Beefy Beans, go to *SJWHandbook.com*). If you don't live at home, look for foods with the descriptor "grown-up ____" as in "grown-up Pop-Tarts" or "grown-up milkshakes" or "marijuana-infused Gummy Bears."

Wage Gapping

As everyone knows, there is a "wage gap" between men and women. For proof, see headlines on *Glamour* and *Cosmo* next to the headlines on sex positions and body positivity tips from Gigi Hadid. Even though many #fakescience studies show the wage gap does not exist if you compare experience and years in the work force, it doesn't factor in *life* experience and circumstances.

Wage Gapping is a food philosophy just for women. It is only eating food that was purchased by men. It's not sexist for men to pay on dates because a woman's purpose is not to be wooed, but to make up for the wage gap. For Wage Gapping, always order more than you can eat so you'll have leftovers for another meal or two. If you have only recently started identifying as a woman, deduct one course from the same number of meals as the number of years you lived as a man. For example, if you lived as a man for twenty years, skip dessert for twenty meals.

Finally, don't let people box you into maintaining a consistent food philosophy. Like gender, your food philosophy can be fluid.

PRO TIP

"For cocktails alone, I figure I owe the male population several thousand dollars. So I will be the one to step forward and say: To the extent one gender is oppressing the other, it's not women who should be complaining."

-Twelve-Time *New York Times* Bestselling Author
Ann Coulter

HOW TO SURVIVE A
HOLIDAY MEAL THAT DOESN'T
FOLLOW YOUR FOOD PHILOSOPHY

Prior to major holidays like Thanksgiving and Christmas, several Social Justice Warrior-friendly news sites like *Alternet*, *Salon*, and *Vox* will offer advice on dealing with right-wing relatives. In an *Alternet* article titled, "10 Ways to Deal with Right-Wing Christian Relatives Over the Holidays," Amanda Marcotte wrote, "There are so many landmines to navigate: Attempts to convert you; arguments about politics; offensive 'jokes' that are really unvarnished bigotry; absurd claims and beliefs that threaten to cause you eyestrain from all the rolling."

Since the topic of talking to relatives has obviously been covered by trusted news organizations, the food is the other aspect of holiday meals where you can show your virtue and educate family and friends on ethical food choices.

Research

If you're going to be in a new city for the holiday meal, do a quick search so you're armed with facts pertinent to your food philosophy. If you're in your hometown, you should already have this information memorized for the times you question the server at local restaurants. Research should include:

- Cost of living so you can deride your host's decision to buy the cheapest eggs
- Locations of Whole Foods, MOM's Organic Markets, or food co-ops
- Local climate and seasonal produce to verify whether a dish served is locally sourced
- Mileage and local gas prices to calculate whether it's better for the environment for them to grow their own kale and other virtue veggies

Declare

- Upon arriving at your host's house, be sure to let them know your allergies, food philosophy, and preferences (gluten-free, dairy-free, vegan, organic, and so forth)
- Remember your "food allergy" doesn't need to be limited to just a physical reaction—it could be an equal or even greater emotional reaction
- If your host asks if you have celiac disease, just say yes to avoid questions about whether you're just avoiding gluten until after Coachella
- Let them know substitutes when appropriate, such as Great-Grandma's Creamy Mashed Potatoes, which can also be made with riced cauliflower

Question

- Just to be safe (you don't want to assume the worst of your hosts), inquire throughout the meal if certain dishes contain any of the ingredients you don't eat.

Example:
You: Does the green bean casserole have dairy?
Host: Yes.
You: Oh. [continue passing around the table while looking at your empty plate and sighing heavily]

- If your host says an ingredient was purchased at a local farmer's market, ask if it was from a local farm or a commercial farm that sells at the farmer's market
- Ask if anyone at the table would like your recipe for Rustic Veggie and Tofu Pot Pie (gluten-free)

Finally, don't forget a host gift. Some suggestions:

- PETA's "Trim Trees, Not Turkeys" holiday ornament
- *Vegan 101* cookbook
- A selection of vegan, fair trade, no sugar treats
- *The Social Justice Warrior Handbook*

PRO TIP

"The people who write those 'how to talk politics at Thanksgiving' pieces have no idea they're the ones their relatives are dreading seeing."

-TV's Andy Levy

HOW TO FORAGE FOR OUTRAGE (I.E., STAY WOKE)

As a Social Justice Warrior, it's important for you to identify every injustice, no matter how small. In essence, you must stay woke. *The Oxford Dictionary* reported the origin of the term "woke" from *The New York Times* article by William Melvin Kelley. In an article on white "beatniks" appropriating black slang, he wrote "If you're woke, you dig it."

Then, in 1972, Barry Beckham wrote in the play *Garvey Lives!*, "I been sleeping all my life. And now that Mr. Garvey done woke me up, I'm gon' stay woke. And I'm gon' help him wake up other black folk."

Then Oxford Dictionary notes, "There are few examples of woke being used with this meaning in public writings in the late 20th century, but woke seems to have made a comeback in recent years. In her 2008 track 'Master Teacher', R&B star Erykah Badu sings "I stay woke," and helps to bring this meaning of woke back into the public consciousness."

To stay woke, we have to be vigilant looking for examples of injustice and cultural appropriation in everyday culture, entertainment, statements, and behaviors. We must demand to be heard and demand action.

TV and Movies

Despite never passing up the opportunity to tell people that we don't have cable or even own a TV, the entertainment industry presents a wealth of opportunities for outrage. Hollywood has been a target for years, so be creative. The website *Refinery29* is the industry standard for identifying outrage in seemingly innocuous things. For example, they were quick to point out that in the trailer for *Wonder Woman*, the powerful superheroine played by Gal Gadot didn't have any armpit hair. *Refinery29* eloquently explained, "It also comes down to freedom. To have or not have armpit hair is a woman's choice and it's one that she's often judged for. With Wonder Woman standing in as an example of female strength, it would have been exciting to see her with a little hair under her arms."

Needless to say, questioning movies and TV for narrowly defining beauty is a good place to start. You can also question the race, gender, sexuality and portrayal of historical and fictional characters.

Music

In May 2017, Social Justice Warriors at a Canadian university were taken seriously after complaining that the song "Walk on the Wild Side" by Lou Reed was played during a university event. The University of Guelph Central Student Association apologized and released a statement saying, "We now know the lyrics to this song are hurtful to our friends in the trans community and we'd like to unreservedly apologize for this error in judgment."

Some other songs to consider banning should you hear them in a public forum:

- "Funky Cold Medina" by Tone Lōc (transphobic)
- "Lola" by The Kinks (transphobic)
- "God Made Girls" by RaeLynn (reinforces patriarchal gender roles and religion)
- "Every Breath You Take" by The Police (creepy, street harassment)

- "Love Yourself" by Justin Bieber (ex shaming)
- "Crazy for You" by Madonna (uses slur for mental illness)
- "Under My Thumb" by The Rolling Stones (sexist)
- "Born in the USA" by Bruce Springsteen (uses the racial slur "yellow man")
- "Boys Don't Cry" by The Cure (toxic masculinity)

Remember that the artist's intent doesn't matter, as the words used could still trigger listeners.

College Campuses

To really hone your Social Justice Warrior skills, you have to think outside the box. With the administrations and professors on our side, it has become quite easy to block conservative and libertarian speakers. Despite their openness to stifling speech, there are still fights to be won. For example, why stop at speech or noise you can hear? Applause is insensitive to those who can't hear. At the National Union of Students conference in Great Britain, attendees were encouraged to use jazz hands instead of clapping so deaf students weren't left out.

The University of Arizona was far ahead other campuses in truly embracing social justice. They presented a plan for students to turn in other students or staff for social justice offenses for $10 per hour. Among the duties of the University of Arizona's Social Justice Advocates:

- "Create an environment that enables Residence Life student leaders to dialogue around topics related to diversity, multiculturalism and social justice"
- "Increase awareness and knowledge of diverse identities and how they influence interactions"
- "Report any bias incidents or claims to appropriate Residence Life staff"

Even though the plan was tabled, we're hoping other institutions of higher learning will embrace and reimagine this program.

> **PRO TIP**
>
> *"Why don't they focus on some of the more important issues? You know, like the potential pitfalls of jazz hands. After all, if clapping excludes deaf people, wouldn't jazz hands exclude blind people? Terribly insensitive."*
>
> –Millennial Kat Timpf

It's tough being a student wading through complex courses such as The Sociology of Miley Cyrus: Race, Class, Gender, and Media (Skidmore College); Philosophy of Phish (Oregon State University); Tree Climbing (Cornell University); Demystifying the Hipster (Tufts University); Wasting Time on the Internet (University of Pennsylvania); God, Sex and Chocolate: Desire and the Spiritual Path (UC-San Diego); and Getting Dressed (Princeton University). Students don't need the added stress that outdated rules and social norms put on them. Here are some other oppressive issues Social Justice Warriors can tackle:

- Library fines for overdue books (Thanks to Harvard for ending this stressful practice!)
- Ethnic foods served in the cafeteria
- Being tested on material that is in the textbook, but not covered in class
- Ethnic foods not being served in the cafeteria

- Display of the American flag (Thanks to UC-Davis/Senate Bill 76 for taking on this fight!)
- Halloween costumes
- Not respecting Muslim students' religious beliefs and traditions
- Prevalence of male school mascots
- Opening of a Chick-fil-A on campus

Kardashians/Jenners

Every day the Kardashian/Jenner women post images and videos on social media that can be used to highlight their problematic behavior and the microaggressions Social Justice Warriors need to fight.

- Cultural/race appropriation: cornrows, Bindi jewelry, Niqab headscarf, Adidas sweatpants, and so on
- Poverty appropriation: oversized clothing, distressed or hole-filled clothing, accepting hand-outs/free products
- Activist appropriation: appearing in commercials or social media posts with hashtags that give the appearance that they care about social justice issues
- Capitalism: using social media as a platform for sponsored content for products they may or may not use
- Wealth insensitivity: posting photos of vacations and private jets despite not traveling to or from a conference on climate change (aka, the DiCaprio Exception)

- Drag queen appropriation: make-up contouring, wigs, overdrawn lips, padding, waist trainers, language (slay, yasssss, queen, fierce, werk, gurl, give a read, and so forth)

Commercials

Our consumerist culture drives the billions of dollars spent on advertising. Like the Kardashians and Jenners, these billions present a bountiful booty of material when foraging for teachable moments. There have been some major advances in inclusiveness in advertising. For example, *Bustle* highlighted a Wells Fargo television ad that "depicts a lesbian couple working hard at learning sign language in preparation for a new arrival from the adoption agency."

It is truly a situation that is inspiring and relatable to all. However, there is always an opportunity to make it better. Why wasn't the couple interracial? Could this have been an opportunity to show that the adoptive child was also transgender?

Even when companies appear to be inclusive, Social Justice Warriors have to keep them on their toes. It's not enough for an ad to show a diverse group of models. Are they doing it because they really think all bodies are beautiful or to sell more body wash?

Common Phrases

Fighting against common phrases that are racist, homophobic, sexist, or otherwise problematic may seem like a daunting task. However, it can be done. In just a few decades we virtually eliminated sitting "Indian style" in favor of "pretzel style" and "criss-cross applesauce." That's evidence that we shouldn't stop there.

Some other phrases to eliminate from public use:

- **Low man on the totem pole** (appropriation of Native American tradition)
- **Powwow** (appropriation of Native American tradition)

- **Gyp or gip** (originated from stereotype of gypsies)
- **Rule of thumb** (originated from men being allowed to beat their wives with a stick no wider than their thumb)
- **Grandfathered in** (not gender-inclusive)
- **Don't drink the Kool-Aid** (reference to mass suicide in Jonestown)
- **All sports analogies** (biased against those who don't follow sports)
- **Moron, imbecile, cretin** (historically used for those with mental disabilities)
- **No can do** (used in 19th century to mock Chinese immigrants)
- **Long time no see** (used in early 20th century to mock Native Americans)
- **You have a pretty face** (implies the rest of a person isn't pretty or that "pretty" is every woman's goal)
- **Blackmail, blacklist, blackball** (all negative words that contain "black")
- **Feminine products** (they are also used by trans men)

As a Social Justice Warrior, the world looks to you to build a more inclusive society by eliminating words, entertainment and people that may cause feelings of discomfort, sadness, or laughter.

PRO TIP

"When you monetize injustice, you can find it under a rock."

–Godfather of Hipsterdom Gavin McInnes

HOW TO PLAN AN
AWARENESS CAMPAIGN

By this point you've settled on an issue you want to bring to the public's attention. Remember that it should be an issue that you are passionate about and that you can exploit for the Social Justice Warrior cause. Follow these steps to maximize your exposure to the media and Social Justice Warrior influencers.

Identify the Problem You Want to Highlight

Think big! It can be racism, sexism, homophobia, anti-Semitism, Ann Coulter is allowed to speak in public, fat acceptance, Islamophobia, increasing the minimum wage, or Trump is Hitler.

Establish Your Expertise

While you could find facts and statistics to back up your issue, this won't help engage an audience. Instead create a graphic that can be shared on social media and retweeted by Blue Checkmark Influencers and other Social Justice Warriors. When designing your graphic, aim for the goal of a retweet/quote tweet with the simple comment of "This" from others.

> **PRO TIP**
>
> *"Thank you, internet. Irony, humor, dank and
> non-dank memes, and so much more. Truly, this is
> an age of miracles."*
>
> -Editor in Chief of Reason.com and
> Reason.tv Nick Gillespie

Share a Compelling Story

Always have your phone with you because you'll never know when you'll be a witness to injustice that perfectly sums up your Social Justice Warrior brand/awareness campaign. You must have pics or edited video or else it didn't happen. A few examples of stories that successfully gained national awareness for social justice causes:

- Gay pastor in Austin, Texas, ordered a cake and was shocked when he picked it up and the baker had written "LOVE WINS FAG" in icing on the cake (2016)
- Muslim woman in New York City attacked by a white man with a knife (2016)
- Africatown Center for Education and Innovation in Seattle, Washington, vandalized with graffiti, including racial slurs, swastikas, and "Vote Trump" language (2016)
- LGBT activist in Cincinnati, Ohio, abducted and locked in the trunk of his car (2015)
- Mosque in Houston, Texas, set on fire (2015)
- Gay man in Salt Lake City attacked and "Die Fag" carved into his arm (2015)
- Lesbian in Baltimore, Maryland, received homophobic complaints because of her yard decorations (2015)

- Bosnian immigrant in St. Louis, Missouri, threatened by three teenagers (2014)
- Black waitress in Tennessee received receipt with racial slurs written by white customer (2014)
- Racist graffiti written seen all over Oberlin College campus (2013)
- Bar owned by gay man in Chicago, Illinois, set on fire (2012)
- Democratic headquarters in Denver, Colorado, vandalized (2009)

All of these incidents perfectly illustrate the racist, homophobic, sexist, and Islamophobic attitudes that exist in America. The events listed above were all cases where the victims performed the actions themselves, but they still helped raise awareness despite being proven to be hoaxes. They were immediately reported and shared by friendly social media influencers and media outlets. The awareness campaign worked because even though they weren't true, they certainly could be true based on our worldview.

PRO TIP

"Victimhood is profitable. On the internet, it can get you thousands of dollars in crowdfunding donations. In the media, it can win you national prominence and a cooing audience of credulous sycophants. On campus, it can get you attention and plaudits from fellow grievance-mongers."

—Gay Icon Milo Yiannopoulos

HOW TO SPOT FAKE NEWS

When we woke up on November 9, 2016, and realized that we were now living in a nightmare in which Donald Trump was elected president of the United States, that was the moment when "fake news" became not just a minor annoyance from following your crazy aunt on Facebook, but an issue of national security.

Unfortunately, the term "fake news" has been hijacked by Trump. In his first press conference after being elected president he said to CNN, the most respected international news network, "Don't be rude. No, I'm not going to give you a question. You are fake news."

Trump and many on the right narrowly define "fake news" as information that isn't factual. However, there are five types of fake news that Social Justice Warriors must counter.

Obama/Clinton Did It

Anytime a conservative or Republican does something that might be legally or ethically questionable, they'll trot out some example from Barack Obama, Hillary Clinton, or Bill Clinton doing the very same thing. This is fake news. You can't compare the deliberate actions of evil people to the same actions of people who are actually speaking for us. Barry, Hill, and Bill don't take multimillion dollar speaking fees from banks and foreign governments because they want the money. They do it for our cause. When right-wing news outlets, commentators, and politicians present this type of fake news point out their racism, sexism, and, in the case of Bill Clinton, that it was just about sex and everyone lies about sex.

X Is a Hypocrite

Too often the right-wing media will try to depict a progressive pundit, celebrity, or politician as out of touch or hypocritical simply because they don't follow the advice they, along with other Social Justice Warriors, espouse. As the DiCaprio Exception states, a person's behavior, net worth, and pretentiousness are overlooked if they identify as a Social Justice Warrior and speak for our cause when advantageous for their career.

Anything That Criticizes Chelsea Clinton

There is no statute of limitations on reminding people that, despite Chelsea Clinton now being an adult who puts herself in the spotlight, kids are off-limits. Period.

Anything That Humanizes the Trump Family

These articles can be the most infuriating because you may see people you think are allies share them on social media. It could be your well-meaning best friend from college who shares a picture of Melania and Barron Trump with the comment, "Politics aside, she appears to be a devoted mother!" By no means should you ever put politics aside.

Fact-Checking That Doesn't Confirm a Hate Crime/Rape

It's very insensitive to share news stories that confirm a suspected hate crime or rape was actually a hoax. It's not just saying that this case was fake, but that all instances of hate crimes are fake. The original report still brought awareness to the issue, which is an absolute good.

HOW TO DO AN *EPIC TAKEDOWN* OF TUCKER CARLSON

In October 2004, social justice ally and vegetarian Jon Stewart appeared on CNN's *Crossfire*. That day inspired us all with the epic truth bomb he lobbed at *Crossfire* cohost Tucker Carlson. Stewart called him "a dick" and told him to "stop hurting America." More than a decade later Carlson is still on TV and hurting America, but there is an important loophole in his mission to silence nonconformist views. Several times a week Social Justice Warriors are able to break through Big Media and speak on Carlson's primetime show on Fox News, *Tucker Carlson Tonight*. Our message of tolerance and social justice is so powerful that even the most powerful name in news can't ignore it.

If you follow the advice in *The Social Justice Warrior Handbook*, it's very likely that you can gain national attention and be invited as a guest on *Tucker Carlson Tonight*. There is no need to be intimidated, shower, or iron your clothes because you have *your* truth on your side. Many Social Justice Warriors have left Carlson stunned silent using this advice.

Agree to the Interview

The first step in planning your epic takedown of Tucker Carlson is to agree to the interview. Some friends and family may warn you against appearing on Fox News. They'll tell you that they'll edit the segment to make you look bad. However, since the show is live and doesn't have produced guest segments like *The Daily Show*, you'll be fine. Be sure to promote the upcoming interview on your social media accounts and mention that you're about to do "a hit" (TV lingo!) on Fox News. Bask in the mentions of your bravery to give you confidence before the interview. Carlson said, "[N]ight after night, some of them come anyway. And we are grateful for that. They may be wrong or misguided, but at least they're not cowards."

Insist on Doing the Interview from Home or a Local TV Station

This is a total power move. By forcing the white, cisgender males who run Fox News to do the interview on your terms you're sending the message that you care more about being in the trenches than being bought and paid for by Big Media. If you're a college student, do the show via Skype from your dorm room or apartment. If you must do from a local TV station, do your own hair and make-up. This segment will live forever on the internet. You want to look like you, not the patriarchy's ideal version of you.

Do Use Props

In a fight, your best weapon is the element of surprise. Using visuals is a powerful way to communicate your message and stun Carlson into silence or laughter. Be creative and don't limit yourself to inanimate objects. Have other stone-faced Social Justice Warriors serve as a backdrop. If you're using printed materials, don't use anything that looks too professional. You want to emphasize that you are part of a grassroots movement. Your prop doesn't need to be aesthetically pleasing. Use fonts like Comic Sans or Papyrus rather than stodgy Times New Roman.

Don't Dumb-Down Your Issue

As a Social Justice Warrior who regularly reads *Vox, Salon, Teen Vogue,* and other progressive thoughtleaders, you are more informed on political issues. It's important to show Carlson and Fox News viewers that you operate on a higher level by using language that may challenge their worldview and comprehension of words they may have heard, but now seem like a jumbled word salad.

Be inspired by this passage from a scholarly article from the *Journal of American College Health* by Kathleen E. Miller PhD: "Sport-related identity, masculinity, and risk taking are components of the emerging portrait of a toxic jock identity, which may signal an elevated risk for health-compromising behaviors."

This article is on the dangers of energy drinks.

Don't Be Specific

Throughout the interview, Carlson may interrupt your peer-researched explanation of a complex issue and ask you to "be specific." This highly aggressive request and attempt to undermine your social justice activism and achievements should not be placated. Instead, spend the remainder of the segment repeating your talking points and asking if you can finish speaking.

Declare Victory

Once video of your interview has been posted, share on your social media accounts. SJW-friendly media watchdogs like *Media Matters* will likely grab the video and help boost your case by saying that you left Carlson speechless or that he defended an untenable position of the right. If there is any question that you didn't win the debate, accuse the entire Fox News organization of ambush journalism and not giving progressives a chance to speak.

PRO TIP

"When your self-image and ego get annihilated on live television, you can't simply admit you have been ridiculous all along. Your brain can't let you do that to yourself. So instead, it concocts weird hallucinations to force-glue your observations into some sort of semi-coherent movie in which you are not totally and thoroughly wrong. That semi-coherent movie will look like a form of insanity to observers."

-"Dilbert" Creator Scott Adams

WHAT TO DO IF YOU GO VIRAL FOR THE WRONG REASONS

As discussed at the beginning of the book, your Social Justice Warrior identity is fluid. At some point during your social justice journey you'll be a Social Media Warrior. Since the newscycle is ever changing, you might be in a situation where a tweet, post, video, or some other content might not be current in the fact it presents. This could include:

- Sharing a parody account of a Republican figure as if it were real
- Not getting a joke that appears to be obvious to everyone else
- Talking about a sexist, racist, homophobic, or transphobic awareness campaign that the right labels as a "hoax" simply because the organizers *performed* the acts themselves and reported otherwise to the police and the media
- Sharing a photo or quote that may have a different interpretation in context
- Misspelling
- Joke about a right-winger's death
- Art depicting a right-winger's death
- Incorrect use of your/you're

Your first reaction might be to delete the post or tweet. However, this will lead to a slew of responses about the deletion and seem like an admission of guilt. Instead, double-down and use it as an opportunity to claim moral superiority.

PRO TIP

"It's 2017. Typos are presidential."

-Author Michael Malice

Change the Subject

If people are pointing out that what you posted is incorrect, change the subject and accuse them of ignoring bad things that have happened.

Example:

Social Media Troll: [Response claiming the wage gap is false]

You: Is it also false that women didn't even get the right to vote in this country until the 20th century?

Name-Call

Under normal circumstances, a Social Justice Warrior wouldn't want to demean anyone, but given that most right-wing trolls are horrible people it's totally acceptable. It should be noted that some words like moron, stupid, and idiot are ableist because they have a history in eugenics (and not the good kind of eugenics promoted by Planned Parenthood founder Margaret Sanger).

Example:

Social Media Troll: It's "you're" not "your"

You: YOU'RE a grammar Nazi, not just a regular Nazi.

Retweet the Trolls

It may seem counterintuitive to give attention to the haters, but it's actually a great way to engage other Social Justice Warriors into piling onto the person calling attention to your post.

Example:

Social Media Troll: That's not true.

You: This person is denying that racism still exists. RT Social Media Troll: That's not true.

Accuse Troll of Changing the Subject

Like Tucker Carlson, many social media trolls may try to engage you in one of the weaker points of your argument or ask for a specific example after you make a sweeping generalization. You're trying to paint an entire group of people as fascist or racist or sexist. They want an example. Hence, they are changing the subject.

Example:

Social Media Troll: Why is it sexist that the remake of Ghostbusters bombed at the box office?

You: You're changing the subject. I'm talking about the toxic masculinity and pervasive sexism in Hollywood in general.

Social Media Troll: Isn't Hollywood run by the left?

You: You're a misogynist pig.

PRO TIP

"Apologize for WHAT?"

-Andrew Breitbart

HOW TO RUIN A HOLIDAY

Americans celebrate a lot of holidays. This presents Social Justice Warriors several opportunities to demonstrate their virtue and others' racism, sexism, and ability to simply have a good time despite the microaggressions all around them.

There are two ways to approach social justice activism and the holidays. You can choose a holiday (Christmas, Easter, Halloween, Cinco de Mayo, and so forth) or choose an aspect of various holiday celebrations that is problematic. The latter offers more opportunity throughout the year to dissect and demand action, so this chapter will focus on that approach. It is not necessary to have any solutions to these issues, but to publicly insist that it's time for a national conversation on _____.

Consumerism

This aspect is easy for Social Justice Warrior beginners. It allows you to take the moral high ground without an overt attack on the holiday, in addition to criticizing the consumption of goods that people don't need that in turn help corporations' bottom line. It's a vicious cycle of demanding more goods, hiring more people to make those goods, and creating more households who can afford to buy more goods. Where does it end?

You can also use this issue for taking a hyper-local stance. Don't buy a Valentine's Day gift for your lover and instead explain that it's an expression greater than love. It's an expression of your social justice activism, which will allow you one day to put a down payment on one of those trendy tiny houses. Remind your lover that they are part of that plan because their car has a trailer hitch and they're the only person with whom you'd want to share 250 square feet.

Inclusivity

Another example that can be used for Valentine's Day is that it is centered on the social norm of a couple. While most people are now accepting of same-sex relationships, there is still a lot of work to be done. Where are the cards for those who are part of a triple? Or the heart-shaped box of chocolates labeled "To My Beloved Bothfriend"? (Bothfriend is the gender-neutral term for a lover who is bi-gender.)

Other holidays that need to do a better job on inclusivity include Mother's Day and Father's Day. The currently accepted celebrations of these days don't include:

- Those who grew up with only one parent
- Those who care for pets, lovers, friends, or coworkers as if they were a parent
- Those who have had an abortion, but who still want flowers
- Those who may not have had the best mother or father and feel triggered by seeing an outpouring of appreciation for others' mothers and fathers
- Those with fathers who don't golf, fish, or drink beer, making it nearly impossible to find a suitable card
- Those who feel pressure from their parents to stop writing books, settle down, and give them a damn grandchild already

Costumes

As Jamia Wilson of Women, Action and the Media told *Refinery29*, "Why do people use Halloween as a time to be offensive?"

Certainly, there are other holidays (St. Patrick's Day, Christmas, Fourth of July, and so on) when people dress up in themed costumes, but Halloween is definitely the most problematic. Every year there is a new pop culture moment that might inspire an offensive costume. Here are some classic costumes that present a host of problems and should be avoided.

COWBOY

While some might look at this costume as classic Americana, it actually represents toxic masculinity, inhumane treatment of animals, and practical use of firearms.

CONSTRUCTION WORKER

Every day women are subject to street harassment by construction workers. By dressing as a construction worker you may trigger women who have traumatic experiences of being catcalled or told to smile.

NATIVE AMERICAN

There are several obvious problems with this "costume." Not only do many who dress as Native Americans attempt to sexualize the identity (a common theme at Halloween), but they also ignore the history and effort behind it. Feathers in a headdress have significance. It has a proud tradition that must be earned, not purchased.

POLICE OFFICER

During these volatile times in race relations, it can be triggering to certain communities to see someone dressed in a uniform they associate with violence.

BIKER

Like the construction worker and cowboy, this costume can trigger strong feelings about street harassment and toxic masculinity. Additionally, Bikers for Trump provided security for right-wing speakers and compromised college campuses' safe spaces.

SOLDIER

For Social Justice Warriors, this is perhaps the worst of the bunch. The soldier glorifies American patriotism and militaristic gun culture. People like Che Guevara have literally died for social justice, so seeing the image of the American soldier in uniform is just not okay.

American Patriotism

Since Trump took residence in the White House (#NotMyPresident), there's been an overwhelming show of patriotism. American flags. Everywhere, American flags! This jingoistic pride in a country with so many flaws will reach a fever pitch on holidays that celebrate American history and traditions, including Memorial Day, Independence Day (more commonly known as the 4th of July), and Veterans Day. These patriotic symbols combined with military hero worship and phallic-shaped meat products make for an abundance of activism opportunities.

PRO TIP

"My anger and hurt feelings when you burn the flag we've fought (and died) for matter less than your freedom to do it. But you still suck."

-Former Green Beret and Master Sergeant in the U.S. Army Special Forces Terry Schappert

HOW TO INFILTRATE A RIGHT-WING EVENT (I.E., PRACTICE TRIGGER DISCIPLINE)

As a committed Social Justice Warrior, you may be called upon to attend a right-wing event. This will take a lot of courage because you will be exposing yourself to new and scary ideas. They won't care about your feelings and may not have your preferred brand of non-GMO snacks.

In order to attend the event without disruption (more on getting an event canceled in another chapter), you'll want to research the event. For an event on a college campus, the administrators often change the venue so that the right-wing student organizers are left scrambling. They also do it to keep turnout low. Check the student organizations' social media accounts for location updates throughout the day.

PRO TIP

"Don't overthink it. A nice button down shirt, a ball cap and a tasty casserole will get you into most conservative events. Remember that to get into most Right Wing Events, you need to know the pass phrase. When attempting infiltration, approach the security posted at the door and say 'I understand the Sheikh is fond of melons.' Remember to look the person in the eye and use a firm handshake."

—Former CIA Covert Operations Officer
Mike Baker

It's very likely that there will be intense security at the event, especially for controversial speakers such as Ann Coulter, Gavin McInnes, Ben Shapiro, Pam Geller, Milo Yiannopoulos, Charles Murray, and Christina Hoff Sommers, among others. Their ideas are so unappealing to free-thinking Social Justice Warriors that violence just seems to follow these speakers. (I mean, have you seen the short skirts Ann Coulter wears?)

Regarding your dress, keep it simple. If you're feeling self-conscious and have visible piercings, borrow a "Make America Great Again" hat. Rest assured, you can purchase holistic sage shampoo to counter any bad energy. There will be no need to cover your face with a scarf or bandanna because you aren't engaging in illegal activity that may get you arrested and complicate your seven-year plan to obtain a BA in Gender Studies.

Once you arrive at the venue, you should be polite to the organizers and security staff. If they're handing out a program or other materials, be civil and say "thank you." While it might make your stomach turn to have their propaganda in your hands, you can turn it in to the school's social justice or hate crimes committee.

For a town hall event with elected officials, be sure you have your talking points from the DC-based social justice organization memorized. You don't want to be seen pulling out a piece of paper that might distract from your concern for whatever town you were assigned that day. Once you're called on, there's no reason to practice "trigger discipline" any longer. As *Refinery29* said, "You can't bully a bully." Regarding town hall events with members of Congress, Alison Leiby of *Refinery29* wrote, "Once in a while bullying has a net positive outcome: Like taking U.S. Representative and iPhone economist Jason Chaffetz down a peg."

PRO TIP

"Unless desiring an advantageous confrontation for media consumption, such as handing out Fair Play for Cuba pamphlets in New Orleans circa 1963, it's best to consult right-wing hate filled screeds' covers. Now knowing your enemy, hit the thrift store for a blue blazer, light blue shirt (red tie optional), khaki pants and oxblood loafers. Thus concealed, while waiting in line, adopt a pensive stare into the distance, as if pondering how to enslave humanity beneath the capitalist yoke. Rest assured, no one at the event will question - or even talk to - you."

—Former Congressman Thaddeus McCotter

If your plan is to disrupt an event from the inside, here are a few ideas:

- Prepare and never waiver from a five-minute statement despite being asked repeatedly for your question
- Turn around and be silent (this will *really* get the speaker's goat)
- Walk out, particularly effective for a graduation event because it shows your commitment to the cause since you're the only one losing stage time

- Lead other Social Justice Warriors in a clever, rhyming chant (I recommend a classic like "Hey hey, ho ho, _____ has got to go.")
- Unfurl a banner with a tolerant message like "Milo is a racist" or "Become Ungovernable"

Before any event, make sure your phone has a full charge so you can get video of any outrageous comments made by the speaker. If you plan on confronting the speaker, enlist a friend to film you.

If the speaker or event organizers try to silence your shouting, loudly remind them of the First Amendment and your right to engage in a dialogue.

PRO TIP

"Unless desiring an advantageous confrontation for media consumption, such as handing out Fair Play for Cuba pamphlets in New Orleans circa 1963, it's best to consult right-wing hate filled screeds' covers. Now knowing your enemy, hit the thrift store for a blue blazer, light blue shirt (red tie optional), khaki pants and oxblood loafers. Thus concealed, while waiting in line, adopt a pensive stare into the distance, as if pondering how to enslave humanity beneath the capitalist yoke. Rest assured, no one at the event will question - or even talk to - you."

—Former Congressman Thaddeus McCotter

HOW TO GET SOMEONE
FIRED OR BANNED

As a Social Justice Warrior, you are committed to equality and justice. This means speaking on behalf of those who don't have a voice by keeping those with whom you disagree from speaking their hateful rhetoric.

Getting someone fired or banned takes the skills of all kinds of Social Justice Warrior identities. Driving others out of the public eye or gainful employment is truly the most inclusive action of our movement's community. Unfortunately, not everyone feels this way. Political squish Bernie Sanders said, "To me, it's a sign of intellectual weakness. If you can't ask Ann Coulter in a polite way questions which expose the weakness of her arguments, if all you can do is boo, or shut her down, or prevent her from coming, what does that tell the world?"

Getting Someone Fired

You've learned how to forage for outrage in everyday things, so now you must translate it to a fireable offense. First, be armed with evidence. If your outrage is based on a social media post, be sure to take a screenshot. Often people realize their mistake right away, delete it, and then post an apology. That doesn't rectify the situation or take away the hurt feelings from the handful of people who saw it before it was swiftly taken down. By having a screenshot, you can continue sharing the offensive material while you whip up outrage.

Armed with your evidence, be it a social media post, photo of a personal item of a coworker that you find offensive, or comment from a professor, contact the person's superior. Communicate that you speak for all who were disturbed, offended, or otherwise made uncomfortable by the target's action. Given that many are afraid to speak out, it is perfectly reasonable for you to claim to speak for a larger group of victims.

Once you have a meeting or social media engagement from the person's superior, exaggerate the damage that has been done. Retweet other complaints while tagging the superior and/ or company. Retweet and tag sympathetic members of the media. Include a hashtag that conveys the action you're demanding (such as #Fire_____) or amplifies the person's small action into a major societal ill (such as #EndLowKeyRacism).

Once you've created a public relations problem within a relatively small social media community, present the case for how this online outrage could translate into a larger public relations problem within a community that actually matters, like clients or customers. Remember that you don't have to demonstrate that business has been lost because of the target's actions, but that it *could*. When someone declares on social media that "I will never shop at _____ again" there is no way to know whether they ever did in the first place. Much like political commentator Ana Navarro being a "life-long Republican" who voted for Hillary Clinton, you can boost your claim (and standing with the media!) by claiming to be a life-long customer.

Once the public relations problem that you've created and nurtured has resulted in at least two hours of no public response from the company, suggest that this could all be fixed if the target is fired.

Finally, after the company has taken the appropriate action and fired the target, insist that it's not enough. Amends must be made via a public apology and acts of contrition, such as an internal review of company policies and hiring of social justice compliance officers who will continue this cycle.

PRO TIP

"This is why the First Amendment is just as relevant in Britain and Canada as it is here. If the people—the culture—don't want free speech, the law isn't worth the paper it's printed on. In Canada and Britain it's illegal to commit thought crimes. You will be bankrupted if you say something that offends the liberal narrative. In America it is perfectly legal to say whatever you want. The government won't punish you, the people will. They'll call your boss until you get fired. The end result is the same in both cases."

-Godfather of Hipsterdom Gavin McInnes

Getting Someone Banned/Uninvited

Many of the same rules for getting someone fired also apply for getting someone banned. Social Justice Warriors have been successful in getting things—books, guns, plastic bags, soda, cigarettes, and so on—banned for years. We now must turn our attention to people. Be creative; you don't need to limit your outrage to just political figures. Comedians such as Jerry Seinfeld, Chris Rock, and Larry the Cable Guy are no longer doing campus gigs because they realize there are some topics that are off-limits in comedy and that list grows every day. Comedian George Carlin once said there were seven words you can never say on television. That list is regrettably short and outdated.

Great strides have been made in the last decade to ban people who annoy or offend Social Justice Warriors. We've been able to get provocateur Milo Yiannopoulos banned from Twitter, several college campuses, and even a conservative event! Likewise, Social Justice Warriors have been extremely successful in getting right-wing speakers banned or uninvited from college campuses.

PRO TIP

"I love [college conservatives] because they're so anti-authority. They love annoying their professors. They love annoying the sort of politically correct status on campus. And apparently, one popular way of annoying liberals is bringing me to speak!"

-Twelve-Time New York Times Bestselling Author
Ann Coulter

Most right-wing speakers are invited to speak on college campuses by right-wing student groups. The key to getting invitations rescinded is to get the school to pull their funding. To do this, you must demonstrate that the speaker has ideas and rhetoric so objectionable that it would result in bad publicity for the school. Additionally, it may expose students to ideas that could challenge their worldview.

If the student group has raised the money required to put on the event or you can't get the funding pulled, your next tactic should be to highlight the violence that these speakers have inspired on other college campuses. Gavin McInnes's invitation to speak at DePaul University was rescinded because the school said allowing it would amount to "public encouragement of violence." The Social Justice

Warriors protesting a speaking invitation to Milo Yiannopoulos caused over $100,000 of damage at UC-Berkeley. UC-Berkeley canceled the speech "amid the violence and destruction of property and out of concern for public safety."

To further incentivize the organizers or the school to cancel the speech, demand that security be hired by the sponsoring organization(s) in order to protect students. Often the cost of campus security, off-duty police officers, and private security can be so cost-prohibitive that the organizers will be forced to cancel the event. School administrators prefer this happen because it's much easier to run an emotionally safe campus than a physically safe campus.

This is the beauty of the "public safety" tactic—Social Justice Warriors are in complete control of whether there is violence at an event.

HOW TO ENGAGE IN A PHYSICAL ALTERCATION FOR SOCIAL JUSTICE

As a Social Justice Warrior, you may be called up to physically fight against racism, homophobia, transphobia, sexism, climate change deniers, and other closed-minded people. I know what you're thinking: "I'm a pacifist, I can't hurt another human being." You're right. It's unlikely that you'll actually hurt someone. That's why you need to learn various techniques and practice so you can boast about being willing to punch a Nazi if you ever have the opportunity.

> **PRO TIP**
>
> *"Punching Nazis in the face is hot right now and the fact that Nazis don't exist has become totally irrelevant. To meet their quotas, they have made "Nazi" mean: any white male who isn't deeply ashamed of himself."*
>
> -The Godfather of Hipsterdom Gavin McInnes

If you're new to fighting, your best option is the sucker punch. This is done when your target least expects it. It minimizes your risk because you're catching the person off guard. Their surprise, regardless of whether it inflicts any pain, will also give you a few seconds to get a head start to run away. If there's a chance the person will catch up with you and punch you back, make sure someone catches it on video so it can be posted as example of right-wing violence against Social Justice Warriors.

If you're hesitant to make physical contact with another person, consider an activity so natural and pure that we all did it as babies: throw something.

Pieing—the act of throwing a pie to make a political statement—has a rich tradition. Canadian activist Pope-Tart (a pseudonym) told the *Les Entartistes' Gazette*, "The pie gives power back to the people because so many feel powerless in the face of big politicians and industrialists."

In October 2004 at the University of Arizona, two Social Justice Warriors attended a speech by Ann Coulter. During her speech they approached the stage and threw pies. They were unsuccessful in hitting her.

Coulter said, "Two liberals responded to my speech at the University of Arizona—during question and answer, no less—by charging the stage and throwing two pies at me from a few yards away. Fortunately for me, liberals not only argue like liberals, they also throw like girls."

Putting aside Coulter's sexist remark that throwing like a girl is somehow inferior, it is true that the pies came nowhere close to hitting her. A recent study highlighted by *The Washington Post* and conducted by the *Journal of Hand Therapy* showed that millennial men's grip strength has decreased from 117 pounds of force to 93 pounds of force from 1985 to 2016.

We must do better.

In the incident at the University of Arizona, it appears that they used cream pies. They could have gotten more distance with a heavier pie because they could have put more force behind it. Better options would have been apple or blueberry, preferably with local organic ingredients. Be warned: non-consensual pieing is considered battery and, depending on whether you hit your target, could be assault.

Of course, throwing pies isn't for everyone. You might choose to hit a non-moving target such as a storefront window, car, or side of a building. This presents many other options for political expression. For objects to throw, consider rocks, trash cans, feces, bottles, or books.

To really get creative, buy the book *A Guide to Improvised Weaponry*. Author and former Green Beret Terry Schappert details how everyday items, such as hot sauce, Frisbees, dirty diapers, and lip balm, can be used to defend yourself against Free Speech fetishists.

PRO TIP

"The two things I understand best are stand-up comedy and martial arts. And those things require an ultimate grasp of the truth. You have to be objective about your skills and abilities to compete in both."

-Black Belt, Comedian,
and Podcast Host Joe Rogan

HOW TO CONNECT ANY ISSUE TO DONALD TRUMP #NOTMYPRESIDENT

While all Social Justice Warriors were #literallyshaking as the election results came in on November 8, 2016, we were also given a tremendous opportunity to use this outcome to champion the cause of social justice.

Toxic Trumpism is the -ism from which all other -isms spring. With the media obsessed with his every move, tweet, and handshake, we must take this opportunity to educate people on how every social, economic, and political ill is Trump's fault.

Heterosexism

At the 2016 Republican National Convention, entrepreneur and venture capitalist Peter Thiel said, "I am proud to be gay. I am proud to be a Republican. But most of all I am proud to be an American."

It is problematic that Thiel felt it necessary to say that being an American was more important than being gay. He should have used his platform speaking in primetime at the RNC to talk about his experience as a gay man. Heterosexism is so pervasive that he probably doesn't even realize he's a victim. Likewise, Chris Barron, founder of GOProud and LGBT for Trump, spends more time talking about the practice in Iran of throwing gay men from buildings rather than how many LGBTQIA people Trump has put in his cabinet. It's time to focus on the real issues here at home! Given Trump's amicable relationship with Democrats, it's entirely possible that he convinced them not to appoint more gays to cabinet-level positions either.

NOTE: Our tactic of shaming businesses into providing services for people despite moral or religious beliefs has been suspended given that many designers have preemptively said they don't want to dress Melania, Ivanka, or Tiffany Trump. In addition to being Social Justice Warriors, we are also conscientious objectors.

Racism

After less than a year in office, all of the racial healing from the Obama Administration has been undone. That's how damaging Trump has been. In fact, many people don't even remember the racial harmony under eight years of Obama.

Sexism

It is so entrenched in our culture that the recording of Trump saying "grab them by the pussy" didn't sink his campaign against the most qualified presidential candidate in history.

Trump's daughter Ivanka's role in the administration is a false flag to divert our attention away from the damage he'll do to women. Every issue can be diverted back to Trump's involvement. Healthcare reform? Bad for women if it doesn't include full-funding for abortion, gender-reassignment surgery, and tampons for trans men.

Climate Change

Climate change deniers are just as bad as multiple gender deniers. We can't even begin to calculate the carbon footprint of Trump, the Trump family, and the Trump properties.

Gun Violence

We already know where Donald Trump stands on gun violence. He is the first sitting president since Ronald Reagan to speak at the National Rifle Association's National Meeting. But what about gun violence against animals? You've heard of the nose-to-tail food philosophy. Well, Donald Trump, Jr. is tusk-to-tail (though the meat is usually donated to villagers). He is an avid hunter of big game. It's also worth pointing out that the meat is donated to a local village without any consideration of the villagers' food philosophies There is only one solution to ending gun violence against animals—arm the animals so they can protect themselves.

Access to Safe Spaces

Trump's presidency has been emotionally, and likely physically, disastrous for Social Justice Warriors. Between parodies, press conference coverage, and must-read think pieces on his tweets, everyone has the right to access safe spaces. In a previous chapter we taught you about creating your own safe space. If there is an impediment to this, such as a magazine cover at the grocery store featuring a bikini-clad woman that makes you question your decision to buy four pints of Ben and Jerry's, you must blame Trump. Case in point: Until 2015, Trump was the owner of the Miss USA pageant, which featured a swimsuit competition.

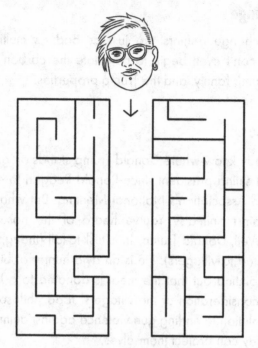

Trump's Fault

HOW TO MANAGE YOUR SOCIAL JUSTICE WORK-LIFE BALANCE

We aren't Social Justice Warriors for the money. As mentioned in the first section, *The Social Justice Warrior Handbook* is for your everyday or hobbyist warrior, not politicians. (For a handbook on using social justice policies for profit, see *Clinton Cash* by Peter Schweizer.)

On Gwyneth Paltrow's *Goop*, Dr. Habib Sadeghi wrote:

"In embryology, there is a condition known as fetal papyraceus: It happens with twins when one fetus grows faster than its sibling, literally starving the other of the nutrients and space it needs to develop. As sad as this scenario is, it can be an interesting way of examining the development of the twin aspects of ourselves: The physical and spiritual."

We can also use this condition to separate our Social Justice Warrior life from the part of our life that doesn't have to be the world's protector all the time. Though we may have a warrior's heart, we have a delicate spirit.

One day you demand the closure of a burrito food truck owned by white people. One day you share a Snapchat story of your *auténtico* three-ingredient mole. It's called balance.

Digital Detox

Do you often find yourself responding to Twitter trolls or scrolling through emoji updates to see if any of them are offensive? It might be time for a digital detox. Before embarking on your digital detox, make a list of your social media accounts and your digital devices. Be honest with yourself! Don't just list your main Twitter account. Also list any Trump children parody or social justice projects accounts you have even if you haven't used them in while. Then decide on an optimal time for you digital detox. Try for a weekend, but if that doesn't fit your lifestyle go for 24 hours (sleeping hours count).

An integral part of any digital detox is letting everyone know you're doing it. Be sure to post on all your social media accounts that you'll be taking a digital detox. During your detox, embrace the simplicities in life. Go on a nature walk. Go to a coffee shop and silently judge the laptop jockeys.

Periodically, it's okay to post an artsy photo to your politically neutral accounts like Instagram with a self-congratulatory hashtag such as #digitaldetox #inspiring #blessed. Remember, the goal is progress, not perfection.

PRO TIP

*"The best way to unplug from social media
is to plug in a Stratocaster."*

-Author and Former Congressman
Thaddeus McCotter

Go Alpha

If you identify as a cisgender woman, going on a campy, traditional date with an alpha man can be a nice change. Take a break from identifying benevolent sexism. Dress in a way that might be appealing to him, but doesn't have a political message. Let him pick you up. Let him hold the door open. Let him pay. Let him walk on the street side without making a statement about it being a vestige of Victorian mores. Then use this perfectly pleasant evening to write a screed about the low-key sexism of a man picking up a woman for a date and telling her she's pretty.

Go to an Adult Summer Camp

A 2017 study by CBS and Nielsen Catalina Solutions found that thirty is the age millennials feel they are adults, which can include paying their own bills and no longer living with their parents. This phenomenon of being thrust into the everyday responsibilities that previous generations achieved at eighteen is called "adulting." Of course, the work is so much more complex, especially for Social Justice Warriors who have the responsibility of cataloguing and countering microaggressions that went unnoticed by less woke generations. In other words, sometimes we just need a break from adulting. Dozens of adult summer camps are springing up across North America because millennials don't need children when they have the attention span of children. Many adult summer camps have land and water sports, open bars, crafts, and nap time.

Take a Mental Health Day

Unlike generations before us, we are totally accessible via Slack, text message, email, Skype, Snapchat, and Instagram for twenty-four hours a day. Because of our constant accessibility and inability to disconnect from work responsibilities, we must take mental health days. Since we were taught that self-esteem is just as important—if not more important—as our skills, we expect our employer to understand that there are some days when we just can't even. While we think you're totally entitled to a mental health day, you may want to refrain from bragging about it on social media. Some employers just aren't progressive when it comes to your right not to work.

Participate in a Nap-In

We all remember those less complicated times in pre-school and kindergarten when it was time to pull out our nap pads and blankets. I had a homemade Strawberry Shortcake blanket from the late 1970s. We needed naps after a few hours of block building and coloring. Imagine how much college students with classes between 10 a.m. and 3 p.m. need them now? At Southern Illinois University, the Morris Library hosted a Dreaming Diversity Art Installation. A student organizer told the school's paper, The Daily Egyptian, "The nap-ins are part of the internal journey to diversity. All dreams start while sleeping."

After your nap, wake up refreshed and ready to lead a protest against problematic school newspaper names like The Daily Egyptian.

Play

Adult playgrounds are popping up across the country. The City Museum in St. Louis, Missouri, has adults-only nights where adults can "take a ride down a 10-story slide, catch a pop-up circus, go for a spin on a Ferris wheel (on the roof!), wander through man-made caves, and order bespoke shoelaces made on a sewing machine that dates back to the 1800s."

Playgrounds aren't just for children. There's no better way to unwind after a long day of dissecting Pepe frogs than at a multigenerational playground. For an extra dose of nostalgia, Instagram photos of your childlike wonder with the filters 1977, Rise and Amaro.

PRO TIP

"If you're interested in 'balancing' work and pleasure, stop trying to balance them. Instead make your work more pleasurable."

-#NotMyPresident Donald J. Trump

HOW TO CONTINUE YOUR EDUCATION AFTER READING *THE SOCIAL JUSTICE WARRIOR HANDBOOK*

As ever-evolving human beings, we are always trying to gain more knowledge and tout our credentials beyond think pieces on *Vox* and *Salon*. (Though skimming think pieces is a healthy foundation of our understanding of complex issues.)

Social Justice Workshops

If you're out of college or focusing on a major that might lead you to gainful employment, there are still several options for workshops that further explore your Social Justice Warrior identity. Northeastern University School of Law held a weekend course on "How to Get It Done." Seminars included:

- Capitalism, Imperialism, and Racism
- White People, Do Better!: A caucus for white people to work together to address white supremacy
- Being an Active Bystander: Learn what to do when you witness bigotry

Western Washington University held a workshop on reducing the impact of white privilege. The workshop was commendably inclusive and was open to everyone. However, they stated that the workshop was most beneficial to white people.

In addition to these special programs available, you may also want to seek out local Social Justice Centers. Wesleyan University has a first-class facility with a proposed annual budget of $200,000. The university's Equity and Inclusion Resource Center includes special resources for students of color, low-income students, female-identifying students, queer and trans students, and first generation students. The budget includes one $800 charcoal grill, but doesn't list the need for a second charcoal grill that is meat-free. Perhaps they'll get more funding in the future.

Confession

This is a fairly new program that's starting to gain recognition. The University of Regina hosted a Masculinity Confession Booth. Hopefully, other universities will follow their lead and expand their confessions to admission of low-key racism and acknowledgment of white privilege. If your city or college doesn't have a confession, you can always volunteer to serve the community by demanding to hear them.

Adulting Classes

First of all, it's not your fault. As The Adulting School says, "You're smart and capable—your education just didn't provide you with all the skills you need."

After spending a summer abroad, a semester in Washington, D.C., as an intern (enduring your uncle's "Monica" jokes to this day), and several course hours on classes about gender studies, there are just some things that weren't covered. That's where adulting classes come in. Some include:

- Traveling in my own country
- Healthy eating
- Improving mood
- Basic laundry and clothing maintenance
- Basic etiquette
- General decision-making
- Reproduction/sex

If you can swing it, you really should insist that your parents pay for these classes. After all, it is part of your education. If they offer to just teach you themselves, just roll your eyes and say "Everything is run by computers now!" That will scare them off.

SJWHandbook.com

Visit us at our online safe space for information, secret tips, and more on honing your Social Justice Warrior skills.

PRO TIP

"The hell of it is, it's not even the students fault; it's our fault. Because we're no longer rewarding logic and reason; we're rewarding temper tantrums. We're no longer focused on justice; we're focused on 'social justice.' We're no longer appalled by violent crime; we save our deepest disgust for 'hate crime.' We're no longer curious about our actual history; we're more interested in revising the past to reflect the things we wish had happened, but didn't."

-Mike Rowe, Host of The Way I Heard It

SECTION 3

Things You Are Entitled to
as a Social Justice Warrior

SECTION 4

Your Social Justice Warrior DreamBook

The following exercises are meant to inspire as you continue your Social Justice Warrior journey.

SOCIAL JUSTICE DREAMS

**Write your hopes and dreams in a non-conformist manner.
There are no judgments and no unrealistic dreams!**

CONFESS YOUR PRIVILEGE

BRAINSTORM WAYS YOU CAN BE MORE INCLUSIVE OF OTHERS

LIST PEOPLE WHO SHOULD BE BANNED FROM COLLEGE CAMPUSES OR BOOKSTORES

PRO TIP

"I believe there's a direct correlation to those who create lists and those who take no risks in life. They don't open a business. They just wait until you open a business and then they complain."

-UC-Berkeley alum
Greg Gutfeld

HATE COLORING

Channel your feelings about Trump here.

THE FASHION-CONSCIOUS CONSCIENTIOUS SOCIAL JUSTICE WARRIOR

Use this space to plan the social justice message you want to convey in your #SelfiesforSocialJustice.

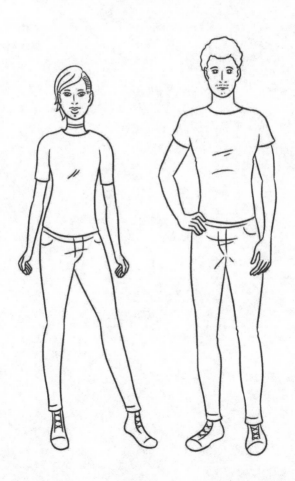

MATCH GAME!

Connect the white, cisgender male host with his anti-SJW crime.
You don't have to use a straight line.
Use whatever feels the most comfortable.

 Displays "Toxic Masculinity" by Opening Show with Sports News

 Posted Artwork Depicting American Flag Without Acknowledging America's Flaws

 Complimented a Woman on Her Appearance

 Talked About Abortion Funding Despite Not Having a Uterus

 Says "Snowflake" in a Derogatory Manner

Answer Key: There are no wrong answers. Go to SJWHandbook.com to print a picture of your trophy!

FREESTYLE YOUR FEELINGS

How did this book make you feel?
What can you do to facilitate a dialogue on social justice issues?
What other books can you read to reinforce your worldview?

ABOUT THE AUTHOR

Lisa De Pasquale is a columnist and author of *The Social Justice Warrior Handbook*, *I Wish I Might*, and *Finding Mr. Righteous*. She is a frequent guest on Fox News and Fox Business.

She is the founder and Monday editor for *Bright*, a daily email for women that focuses on culture, lifestyle, and national news. She writes a regular interview feature for *Townhall.com* and is a contributor to *The Federalist*. She was director of the Conservative Political Action Conference (CPAC) from June 2006 to April 2011.

De Pasquale has authored articles for *The Federalist*, *Washingtonian*, *The Daily Caller*, *The Washington Times*, *The Houston Chronicle*, *Townhall Magazine*, *Broadly*, *Breitbart*, *The Guardian*, *Human Events* and the *Tallahassee Democrat*. In 2010, she was named a "Rising Star" by *Campaigns & Elections* magazine in their annual list of top political leaders under 35.

Follow her on Twitter at @LisaDeP.